Poets' Corner
2020

The Bayside Writers' Group

Copyright © 2020
The Bayside Writers' Group
All Rights Reserved
ISBN: 978-0-6485152-8-9

This publication may not be reproduced, stored in a retrieval system, or transmitted in whole or in part, in any form or by any means, electronic, mechanical, photocopying, recording, or otherwise without the consent of the author(s). Inquiries should be addressed to the publisher.

Published in Australia
Printed by Ingram Spark

Poets' Corner 2019 Authors: Amanda Divers, Ann Simic, Elizabeth MacGregor, Judith Dowling, Maxim Anderson, Peter Levy, Rose Crane, S.G Lanteri, Suzanne Siebert.

Design: Sharon Hurst
Uploads: Alex Nutman a.e.nutman@gmail.com

Acknowledgements:

I would like to thank all those who took the time to submit their works to us. Please note that if anyone would like to make contact with any of the poets in this collection that the best way would be to either post a letter:

The Bayside Writers' Group
22 Stradbroke Avenue
Brighton East, Victoria, Australia 3187

Or email:
baysidewritersgroup@bigpond.com

Contents

Amanda Divers

    Australiana 1
    She 13
    Alumni 24
    Sunflower 34
    Red 45

Ann Simic

    Escape from Crow Road 2
    Peace 15
    A villanelle for the library 25
    Beasts of the night 35
    Parroting in lockdown 46

Elizabeth MacGregor

    Kitchen cupboard 4
    A stranger's key 14
    Busy beavers 18
    A new day 28
    A wallower 47

Judith Dowling

    Deleted 3
    Sunday market 16
    The biographer 26
    The celebrity 36
    This crowded train 48

Maxim Anderson

- A sacred land 6
- Each day can be a miracle 19
- Teeth of the reaper 29
- A closed off world 40
- Eyes of the dead 50

Peter Levy

- Everybody lies 7
- How near you are 20
- I long for the gardens 30
- Dress me in old Europe 41
- A clock watcher 51

Rose Crane

- Earth says hello 12
- Valley of wine 21
- Complex origami 31
- For I love many 34
- Words from ethereal 42

S.G. Lanteri

- A statement of damage 8
- Double take 22
- Ending 32
- Stolen 1910- 1970 43
- Red is the color of your eye 55

Suzanne Siebert

- Gallipoli 10
- Sun 23
- Brother 33
- Blue places 44
- Charge 52

Australiana

Holding hands I slowly see, everything I know they can be
Strawberry fields and blood orange trees
Golden Sunsets, and Riddles Creek pie
They'd hold each other under every night sky
And people in the town would say,
How they hoped and wished they had their way
For you've never seen such a love in your life
Compared to that of the love of the farmer and his wife.

Amanda Divers

Escape from Crow Road

It was the day her grandmother exploded
that she folded her clothes and closed
the door with a deep-throated sigh.
The sky screamed in a purple rage
but the cage door was open for her to fly,
to splice the straightjacket of despair,
to tear from the demon's dirty lair
into the jaws of freedom, the rhythm
of the unknown far from madding gran's
menacing strife, rife with malice
into the arms of Persephone perhaps
in Hades with the promise of Olympus:
the ways of freedom are not safe
but happiness is worth the chafe.

Ann Simic

Deleted

I was deeply in love with a Poem last night
Willing to take it for better or worse.
My Poem and I both had fluttering hearts
As we shared our most intimate thoughts
Together we churned the bedclothes
As words of devotion poured out.
I lay wrapped in the arms of my Poem
'Oh Lovely One, you are my delight,
I adore your every word.'

I woke late on the morning after,
Booted up, and searched for my poem
There it was, filed under 'Romance'
But after I'd read it over, I knew
Poem was just not my type
So it gave me the greatest pleasure
To simply press- with a florish, 'Delete'

Judith Dowling

A kitchen cupboard

A kitchen cupboard opened squeaking
And I, with patience, closed it.
But could not stop a thought from leaking
Through a portal deep within
A squeaking door that tells a tale
Of love and pain that all could share
I touch the cupboard door and see
More than a man in love could bear.
Those thoughts of love lost from my heart
Misplaced, though not forgotten
Feelings hurt and torn apart
That never did get mended.
And how changed I have been
To play a stranger's sport
Forever locked in time and scene
A victim to this thought.
A kitchen cupboard loosed once more
And I, with patience, close it.

A kitchen cupboard opened
And I, with patience, closed it again
But I could not stop a thought from drifting
Through a portal deep within
A squeaking cupboard door, so full
Of memories that one should share
And yet, inside, this need remains
Alive and more than a man could bear.
This pain that lingers
Never will mend
And how changed I've been

As a stranger to the end.
Forever locked in time by this
I carry a victim's stain
The cupboard opened once more
And I, with patience, close it again.

Elizabeth MacGregor

A sacred land

In a sacred land
That most would call a desert
An empty space of infinity
Holds a glorious parade

Unworldly beasts will plummet to Earth,
Bringing with them holy treasures and priceless riches

Their huge bodies swaying in the windless air,
Their legs taking slow steps-
Must be careful when carrying such precious things...
Slowly, steadily, heavy breathing, careful

They are not blinded by the golden rays of Heaven,
Shining in their eyes.
Gentle but strong are the beasts
As is the man who commands them

Trumpets blare as he conducts a storm of gold,
Head high, a heart beating like an orchestra of drums,
As he watches in pride at his marvellous work
Held in an empty space of infinity,
A place that most call a desert,
A sacred land

Maxim Anderson

Everybody lies

We all do it
It's the one thing we all have in common
Like a curse, pushing us into the abyss
Sometimes, most times, self endorsing
"I did it to protect you"
Protect me!? From whom and what?
But I do it too, we all do it
Hypocrites to the end
Words turn back into just that, words
And the meaning of life is somehow lost by it
Religions and countries thrive on it, calling it faith and duty
How convenient and trite
As if a judge and jury would play by a same rule
It's all about survival in the best condition
Where ends justify the means
Where means is that little white thing
And it really is no big deal
We all do it, everybody lies.

Peter Levy

A statement of damage

Yesterday
after the fire of innuendo,
we went to see the skeleton
of the old church of secrets
Vacant rose tracery
perforated walls, exposed ribs
blackened cross stark against pale blue heaven

In the smoke-hazed air
we slowly sensed those around us
silent people of a certain age
standing close-cold in their own memories
witnessing
at various points of vision
different types of destruction

We returned each day
to document the church's journey
Its nuance into another reality
into its changed vocabulary
and to grasp what it had to say

On the fourth day
closed off behind crossed barbed wire
we found it alone
all the hullabaloo of the curious
the amazed, and the saddened
had gone
and save for an occasional car
slowing as it went by
it seemed this burning was already stale news

And as it had nothing to disclose
we too left it to the multiple contradictions
held within its now blackened heart

S. G. Lanteri

Gallipoli

Even before the battle began
Too many of them hadn't even had their boots touch the shore
Not knowing their last breath was actually blessed, as they washed in tide and drowned
The wounded lay, screams of murder curling and landing on the foreign ground
The air became a warfare purgatory with 'fatal' just either rushing past, or quickly claimed you dead
The game of will and survival had changed – this the day all the lads became honoured men
Moving in terror they went across to wherever 'safe' was declared
You made it fast before you lost your will or lost your leg
This was the devil's playing field – with angels witnessing the black and red of death
Whatever you do, don't let the older men know just how desperately you wanted to go home
Even they, too, held this prayer, only God knew it was said behind a frightened breath
Along with 'let this day be over', give me the strength I don't already know I own
The first time you pulled the trigger, you became not just a man,
You had become a 'digger,' who would later wear medalled ribbons upon their aging chests
As the world saw it in black and white, there was only one colour Anzacs saw for years
It was red; it ran through their veins, stained the soil and stung their tears

Lives were blurred by what was done, what was to come, and who lay before you dead
A whisper made at dawn, with a sky clouded by those who mourn,
The bugle claims the song of the soldiers, who went to heaven too soon and lived in hell too long
Honour the man, who gave his heart, braved each hour and came to be an Anzac
For their legacy and their remembrance are our dues to tell

Suzanne Siebert

Earth says hello

We live with trees, we live with the plants, we live with all the species and that is how it is meant to be.
I found it in the park across the way.
A part of a tree and just one part of it.
The essence and quality of a piece of wood, observing it as I picked it up, like a joint and socket, twisted and bound through the years it took to grow.
How they grow ever so slow intermingle they do which makes it even more such a wonder.
Earthy and a bit mysterious, so we can all try to figure it out and how it is meant to be.
For how nature forever leaves its clues for us to follow.
For the earth speaks a language of its own.
Do you hear what it has to say?
Do you understand?
Do you hear its calling?

Rose Crane

She

The truest you the unkempt and wild
She was the constant poet
While you watched others scramble to piece words together
Full well knowing it could never be
The standard in which you speak
The truest you looking at the truest me
Eye to eye in contact
Our reflections mirrored perfectly.

Amanda Divers

A stranger's key

Sometimes I misplace things
And, as if they didn't matter, forget them.
People's names and places
Lost inside a complication that is me.
Yet, you see me as one who finds things
And there is truth in that I can
As long as I am able to juggle what I want to see
I amble selectively, in rhythm on a plan.
I see others' keys at restaurants
Or glasses resting by a fireplace on a chair
So easily misplaced and left
And I never resist the urge to care.
How full of pride I am to be the one
Where an opportune moment's collision with fate
Can assist the weary stranger's load
Beholding gratitude once more on my plate.
And can I remember flowers
When a day has been quite void of love
Sometimes I do, with good reward
But, in truth, I do not do these things enough.
How important is a stranger's key
When compared with my own
When simple words and gifts from my soul
Will heal the hearts of those close, who feel alone.
I see much and misplace more
As a victim of complacent coming age
And how differently do we act out our roles
Within our loving home and stage.

Elizabeth MacGregor

Peace

The florist told me it's very hard to kill
the peace lily. Indoors or outdoors,
much or meagre water, it survives all
situations. A plant for all seasons.

I bought it because it pleased my spur of the
moment itch. I notice now one leaf has a
cut in it, another is slightly deformed, the buds
about to open are wrinkled, the fully-fledged

ones are smooth, raise heads to the heights
like fairy-wrens. One leaf is striated white
and green, the rest shiny pickle-shamrock-emerald
stalks stand straight or softly sinuous.

Yesterday, a cat killed a fairy-wren in the garden,
guarded it triumphantly on the doorstep.
Now, only a few feathers, spindly legs and claws
remain, gathered in a dish beside the peace lily.

Ann Simic

Sunday market

I watched a pretty girl with Fairyfloss hair
Twiddling and twaddling
Shiny stones, beads, and odd bits and bobs
Wire and wood and metal shapes
Things you might find in your great grandmother's boxes
Or perhaps in another world
 All flashing here and there and roundabout
Obeying her little hands.

'What are you making and
Did you make all these beautiful things?'
She held up a thing called a Do Dah
So rare, the only one of its kind
She said the small ones were Thingamajigs
The larger ones were called What Its
They all winked at me, flashing beautiful smiles
Which lit up the day with their shine

She hummed as she twisted, tugged and tied
Wrapping so deftly, in over and through
As her strong little fingers bickered away
In a language only she knew.
'What's this?' I said, 'It's perfectly lovely'
As I scooped one into my hands
'Be careful, it's precious', she said to me
'It's a Wigwam for a Goose's Bridle.'

It was something I'd always searched for
I found it hard to believe my eyes

It was just what I'd dreamed of all my life
 But thought I'd never find
I wanted to kiss the Fairyfloss girl
For creating this magic for me
She told me that if I bought it
And polished it every it every day
I'd be loved forever
Which was a secret I always knew
How could I resist?
Would You?

Judith Dowling

Busy beavers

What busy beavers we are
With new toys and games
To touch and smell
A rose by newer names.
To live in this way.
We say is civil and free
Yet both these words seem strange
To you as well as to me.
For whom do we serve
The purpose is not clear
Too many words confuse me
With such doubts within such fear.
No time to waste in idle sport
Where battles win and lose in thought.

Elizabeth MacGregor

Each day can be a miracle

Each day can be a miracle
Or a step toward euphoria.
With the right dedication and effort,
The entrance to your personal heaven can home you in no time

Each day can be a disaster
Or a fall to the curb.
With lack of dedication and effort
The void into a grey abyss can home you in no time

Some nights I cannot sleep-
Too proud of myself
With my recent productivity and success, and excitement for the future

Some nights I cannot sleep-
Too disappointed in myself
For letting plentiful yet valuable time escape and malnourish my future

Some days plant seeds for my life ahead of me
And make me want to live forever

Some days make me fear what lies ahead
And make me wonder if it is worth living at all

Maxim Anderson

How near you are

How near you are, while all lie sleeping
With careless dreams, to share the night.
To rest young hearts, from all confusions
Peaceful, yet still, full in flight.
Each day a quest, to answer questions
Quelling doubts, that linger on.
Each discovery, such adventure,
Simple deeds, that need be done.
Today is gone, with much to ponder
I can but marvel, their will to see.
Those wondrous sights, so lost in wisdom
By all of us, especially me.
My inward light, will guide your footsteps
Shining gently, through your hair
So near you are, my thoughts can touch you
Across the darkness, breathe your air.

Peter Levy

Valley of wine

How tempting the wine from the valley with the views to please.
There that day planting the seeds that grow the trees and the future of better things with my hands in soil, rich and earthy.
Though it was cold, the sun would shine through and brighten my heart and how it would warm my body and soul.
The place in a valley with the views to please and how tempting the wine with its taste and tones of fruity, earthy, robust.
I could not drink that day for I was there to plant the seeds for a better tomorrow with trees and wishes to please.
For I wonder do people understand the importance of seeds that grow the trees and the future of better things?

Rose Crane

Double take

My home is hollow
Your heart is fractured
A perfect duo
in a modern world

I'm piano played
putty malleable
limp ragged
tin taut
my mouth a cavern
vocal yet dumb
as dishonest as you
pulling the strings

I am you
You are me
but when the curtain drops
the performance over
I'm doubled up, cased inward
and you go
free

S. G. Lanteri

Sun

"Take me where I can see the sun,"
"No child, there is no need to see the sun.
It's shining all around you child."
"Can I keep the sun?"
"No child, you cannot keep the sun,
For how could others see you without it?"
'There's no need for the sun for us to see,"
"Why do you say that child?"
"Because I'm blind, and I can see everything."
"Why do you want the sun then child?"
"To teach you all to see without it."

Suzanne Siebert

Alumni

Here I stand, the names trickling down my spine
As a haunting reminder of what was
Thirteen years on, I smile, I pull on this comfort I denied so long ago.
I sit, I think of all ways I have changed, how better I am now.
I wonder.
They are not the people I knew, they are better, they are stronger, they are wiser.
I will not shrink inside myself, they have grown.
I pull on this comfort and smile, knowing the names spread across my back are those of strength and courage.
Of those caught between traditionalism and hope.

Amanda Divers

A villanelle for the library

Everything was quiet that day
but for the whispering of books
in the library where they lay.

Sleeping or just looking fey,
resting in their private nooks;
everything was quiet that day.

How long would that silence stay,
casting forth its languorous looks
in the library where it lay.

It cannot last is what we say,
softer than the babbling brooks;
but everything seemed quiet that day.

A book on war began to stray
with its retinue of crooks;
we could not find where peace now lay.

What is the price that we must pay
for the hush that cleaves its hooks;
but everything seemed quiet that day
in the library where books lay.

Ann Simic

The biographer

Whatever happened to the Ugly Sisters?
Well may you ask!
Ah ha! You'll have to read my biography
I'll tell you this much-
The truth, only the truth.
Firstly there's Violenta
The elder one, that's me
I suffered an awful breakdown after the wedding
After that cleaning girl Cindy flaunted herself,
Wed that fabulously rich newspaper mogul
And drove off in a solid gold Ferrari
Wearing crystal stilettos studded with diamonds.
It should have been me!
I eventually got over the mogul
I bought (thanks to Mummy)
A nice little business in undies
'Ladies Intimate Apparel'
Knickers , bras, teddies and such
For footballer's wives and footballers
It was all a huge success
Considering I once got an axe through my head.
Truth, truth. Let me see
Let me behold it before my eyes
It's not that I was ugly at all
Oh no, no, no
All that was just a symbol
Of what a terrible childhood can do.
Some upstart reporter got it wrong.
Poor Mummy
Even before her rigor mortis

Daddy married that pathetic woman
And of course she had to produce
Their damnable Petronella
She was only a half and so ugly
Drove a Porsche at twelve
To Monte Carlo on Saturday nights
Read all about it.
And here's another snippet or two
She, the little half, Petty, got the wrong man
Four times
She ended up in cement (thanks, to husband three)
After the lobotomy failed
After she'd snipped off her ten little pinkies
With Daddy's secateurs.
My own research shows that Cindy
Fell off her shoes and lost both her feet
The mogul? Ha! He lost all his hair.
I've a man who's going to marry me
After my next face lift he says.
For now I stand in the tower of a luxury McMansion
With binoculars - scanning the sea.

Judith Dowling

A new day

A new day has dawned
The sun is shining bright
Birds fly through the sky
The moon remembers the night.
A dog barks in the distance
My eyes moisten and stare
In wonder at the new day
Shivers race through my hair.

Elizabeth MacGregor

Teeth of the reaper

Whether you're a gold loving king
Or a dirty street sweeper,
A sunshine orbiting figure of joy,
Or a suicidal weeper,
Whether you're the kindest bird flying
Or a nefarious creature
We all taste the same
Between the teeth of the reaper

Maxim Anderson

I long for the gardens

I long for the gardens where
Once there was one
That lived in some vision
Of times long since gone
What does one expect of me
That I could do that too
To heed that call, within, beyond,
That flows so harshly through.

Peter Levy

Complex origami

Came the unfolding of a complex origami reminding of us of just how to be.
To be simple like the beauty of a flower but almost as strong and flexible like a tree with roots so deep and branches that sway in the wind.
For it is time to listen to the wiser one from the mountains so high.
Through the years with the spoken or unspoken words that had almost crippled and numbed the soul.
It was time and the night had brought its magic to the one whose turn it was to change, given a new life with symbols and messages from the ones that that passed and from the ones that know better.
A life that is true and a life that is meant for you and that is how you will get through this complex not so true world.

Rose Crane

Ending

For so long good neighbours
So careful, so sure they had been
yet it was the smallest of gestures
small but significant
spontaneously removing a hair
from the shoulder of another woman's husband
that gave them away
A gamble lost

Feigned love as subterfuge for their hidden music
Such commonplace betrayal for so long
and no guilt
Such voices harsh at this denouement
Such salt on the tongue

How far have they come?
How far have they strayed from their former selves
when even their shadows cringe on ownership?

No love in this double ending

S. G. Lanteri

Brother

"Above all, to thine self be true"
You are in kin and in kind
You are by me, half a world is not enough to prevent
You are the strength in my hand

And you are the words said of care of mine, of first, of now, of ever
I would have thought less of me, in spaces only I could see
And you healed them all, with great reverence, so don't deny favour, or choice or chance of goodness to come in life
After the dark, and sky becomes time

Speak clear, in clarity, in respect for one and more, the other
So, I stand beside my fine brother
Spirit of beyond whatever moves the moon
We connect by her eye

Until I see with these eyes,
My heart rests in places,
I am yet to take to,
And will in time.

Suzanne Siebert

Sunflower

If she was a flower, she would be a Sunflower
Golden and fresh, tender to the touch
An aromatic blessing, a smile without smiling.
A hug without touch, a brightening beam of sunlight
with comfort as such.
If she was a flower, a Sunflower she would be
Happy brightening everyday living life so endlessly.

Amanda Divers

Beasts of the night

Nestled in the perfect cocoon of
pillow and cover, ready to drift off,
pictures stream through my DVD mind:
the doleful child entreating reprieve,
the refugee shunned offshore by
pontificating pollies proud to stop boats
and destroy lives. Stop the tape,
let me off the hook, I've done all I can.

I've got up with GetUp, I've emailed and rung,
now I covet my cocoon, but like an LSD spider
web in disarray, I'm a jumble of tossed and
turned irritation that camomile and
valerian can't combat.

I'm not sure about the velvet night any more.
It used to be so dependable. Now it
leaves me sleepless. All night I write
unreliable memoirs in my head
in my bed of nails and roses.

Ann Simic

The celebrity

Departure time is eighteen o ten. I'm late and the custard's gone lumpy
Slam it in the blender? Shove it on to high? Give it to the cat and start again?
Lumpy custard! Tongues will swell and throats will throb with fire
Each mouth will give birth, in its own unique way, to a roll of rusty barbed-wire
I've paid the bill re. repairs to the tents, forty nine dollars and fifty nine cents
I'm confident, talented, needed.
I've rung for a taxi. Straight ahead, airport please. Straight ahead, not left not right
Arrange the seating for the wretched scout meeting. I'll suggest a lamington night
The flight's on time which is really grand. I hate being late for meetings
I've got my report in my cool little hand. I've balanced my books. I've succeeded!
I've fed the dog, signed a contract or two. Got my little red book so I'll know who's who
And baked the scones for the supper.
Got my itinerary, passport, tickets and cheques, plus the roster for making the cuppa.
At Kennedy Bruno will drape his Astrakhan around my shoulders' Hawaiian tan
While I suffer Roderick's kiss then clutch Franz' hand for support.
And poor dear Larry will try to be brave as he looks at me with the eyes of a slave

While the scout master reads his report-
His khaki shorts lap over his socks and his hat's at a very odd angle
Impeccable creases, freshly shaved but you see strange sights in Manhattan
He says the Collins' boys are better behaved and talks of plans to construct a trench
I look up at Franz, hold both of his hands while I tell him I love him, in French
Meeting Kim in LA. Ah what a delight. She'll be there in the tuck-shop at seven ...
Vegemite rolls, all fresh and white. It seems white's the color this season
Yes I'll give them a shock, I'll wear my black. No I'll wear the red, there's always a reason.
It's completely scattered with studs at the back and there's not much at all at the front
I just hope I don't clash with the carpet.
After recess time I'll call in on Trish. She could be like me but she hasn't the wish
Must return the dish that I borrowed last month, for our annual gala kindergarten lunch
I'll hand on Tom's jeans, hardly worn, just outgrown. Ye gods how time has just flown
And then I must rush to avoid the riff-raff, cheering fans all wanting my autograph
While I'm in Boston delivering a lecture (Theo Fletcher, MIT, Thursday am)
I must help Gerry with his latest conjecture on Edgar Allan Poe
When I've talked with Max Hoarie, (he wants my life story)
I'm due at the White House for dinner. I can't let them down

They're announcing the winner and of course they're expecting a pav.
I cut up the blinking butter beans
I can't tell you just what it means to think of you eating the flaming fruit flan
Waiting there for you in its non-stick pan
I'll be home by nine thirty, but I might be late
Maybe six weeks from tomorrow
I'm not sure of the date
I can't help it, I'm sorry, I'm needed
I'm called for, I'm great.
 The Fosters from Elm Street are awfully nice people. Little Toby's so utterly sweet
 They've asked us away, first week in June, somewhere out west for the brass band contest
And though I know it's a marvelous show, I'm far too busy, can't possibly go
I'll be in Cannes for the Fest
I simply must join Ben, jasper and Chad for a week on the "Starlight" at sea
They can't start the film without me.
Chad of course is young Michael's dad,
The ambulance driver, who seems very glad to test for the first-aid badges
And Jasper, is the brilliant director recently transferred from the bayside sector
Handsome Ben is so tall, with shoulders like boulders tells me my eyes drive him crazy,
So although arrangements are somewhat hazy I've invited him home for the Easter Parade.
And when that's done we'll relax in the shade before we nip off to Cowes, for the penguins
Then to Queenscliffe of course to visit the fort.

Oh it'll all be so wildly wanton and Ben will doubtlessly say, too short!
Memo – Talk to Katherine re Academy Awards
I'm speechless I'll say and I love you all
Then I'll race right out as the crowds applauds
Just for a minute to give you a call
As I dab the tears from my eyes
And suggest cheese and bickys in the scout hall
If we charge a bit extra, I'll wisely surmise
We'll have those new tents in no time
Beaming in at ten thirty to sign for the homework
You might just be silently dreaming
Forgive me my Darlings
For my vocation
It's not easy at all when on location
I'll look down at you though the flight may be bumpy
And laugh at you screaming
"This custard is lumpy"
Hello International Lost Property?
Please would you be so kind
My name? Yes my name is Sandy
Now just a minute I might be Mandy
I'm not quite sure, I could even be Andy
Yes. I remember, I'm Mahatma Gandhi
I've just got in on a flight from Nandi
And I seem to have lost my mind.

Judith Dowling

A closed off world

In a closed off world,
Overrun with fear,
Attacked with contagion,
Some are no less than trapped in their homes

With the calamity of society on hold,
The skies clearing,
Nature rebuilding,
Some have an opportunity

Time goes by, wasting away,
Life drains and the mind is infected,
Infected with misery,
Knowing the festivities that can be no more

Time is plentiful, and to be used wisely,
Life goes on and the mind can learn,
Learn new expertise,
Knowing festivities can wait

Lockdown can be a curse. It can also be an opportunity.
Life does not change. You have to be the change.

Maxim Anderson

Dress me with old Europe

Dress me with old Europe's charm
In etiquette and mannered walk
Accepted, yet so hidden, guilt
Confusing innocents in talk.
Old enemy, that speaks of peace
As if we miss the cultured hand
Again so slight in history's name
Mistakes we still don't understand.
Such seeds are long inside this soil
Winners write and lay all blame
Always on the other sides
As is the nature of this game.
Perhaps my eyes now see a truth
And maybe veils can lift and be
But how can I compare a dream
With life, that is reality.

Peter Levy

Words from ethereal

The words of a faraway place but close to your heart.
The warmth of words, the harshness of words.
The words of the ethereal in our minds.
How they answer the questions that may be troubling us.
What to do and what to say?
Why?
For you may need those words one day, to save your life or another.

Rose Crane

Stolen

1910-1970

When we hear
the intruders coming closer,
crossing our tracks
run quickly dear children
Hide well
When their wheels have gone
we will find you

Hold tight your memories
our language, stories, song, dance
Hold tight your belonging
Lest you forget

S. G. Lanteri

Blue places

In cold darkness, in an empty room
A new place, an old soul, newly broken ten years ago
I'm taking time to find some
Wanting more than just a moment, to create some

And in the alone of a place called home
Where we were before you weren't
I'm waiting, for the right one
From and in amongst all the every and any things

Saddened blue eyes, blue, seeing not beyond them
Without light for distinction, or dimension
No navigation, not knowing nor with any sense of any of
the many directions

So as I make my words, so silently as you read them
With all of night's dark hardness surrounding me
After burying what isn't there; my only, my one, my
heart, my hope, my other part of me
Am I breathing for a reason or wanting to find one?

The door stays closed to those I know
Sitting still, still sitting in the same blue chair that was
blue during the day
Hours pass counted only by heart beats
But only every second time
It's trying to live on its own.

Suzanne Siebert

Red

The skies are neon red
Families are feared dead
It's not a swift pull or a deadly spike
More like a trickle of loss burning inside
If only we could use the tears we have shed
Let it cleanse the earth and revive what is left
Families are torn, the nation is lost
They say help is coming, but what does it cost?
The lands are littered with corpses of the animals from our crest
Humanity is trying, we can only do our best
We've put in so many hours, it's been sleepless nights
But if there is one thing I'm sure of, this country knows how to survive.

Amanda Divers

Parroting in lockdown

We could be seeking eclectus parrots in the Cape York wilderness. Walking and stopping, stopping and walking.
Imagine her, scarlet, blue-breasted, billowing black beak.
Imagine him, electric green, red under wings, orange beak;
so different but equally dazzling, hidden in the rainforest,
recognising each other. Other-worldly. We chance upon them,
a gasp of luck. Nesting, she sits and waits and watches,
occasionally ringing her metallic, melodious bell,
cut crystal in the air. No partnering response, he sits
in the impassive branches, while we wait and wait and wait.
Anxious, she flies to him, confers and returns to her hollow.
A final clear-cut call and he joins her.
Patience and persistence pave the path
in such affairs of state and heart.

Ann Simic

A walllower

I once cared little of time and love
Yet now drown in them each and every day
As if all life, that held no more reason,
Suddenly within, shrouded in mystery.
And then come those minor chords that choke
With the yearning of weakness to hang on and hold
Collecting thoughts and passing glances of strangers
On this mission to observe some life unfold.
Like I've waited eternally in some blind faith
For you to be the one that freed me
To exist *wallowing* in your essence
Yet in prison. Nothing more to be.
Nothing nailed to fear, nothing left to forgive
Still one step on another to live.

Elizabeth MacGregor

This crowded train

On this crowded train
I am looking at people
(I like to look at people)
On this crowded train I am stripping them of their clothing
Enjoying the contrast of bulbous arcs with gentle curves....
Bending, stretching, slumped and slouching
One hundred pinkish-brownish-grayish contortions
Grotesque and also beautiful
A vision abstracted from ordinary vision
The maps around their lips,
The wind-up keys in their ears
And their holland-blind eyes in curfew
What occupies the rooms of their heads?
I am looking at people
Eyes blank to the windows kaliediscopes
Rocking and rolling until they're to lose their minds
Rattling forward knowing there's no going back.
Or so it seems.
Hands are turning pages
Or massaging one with the other
Maybe they think, am I alive? Can I feel?
Hands knitting without knowing
The swing of straps hypnotizes.
Then one by one heads drop and loll on the floor
Where they can't fall any further
Then the black tunnel hits
Like a cruel stoke to the brain
The train ambushes the station

Bodies are clad
Clocks tick again
With doors agape and realities found
From deep down under seats
They pour from the train in globules.

Judith Dowling

Eyes of the dead

He wanted nothing more than to end it,
The everlasting burden like a knife in his cold heart.
He had been cursed with a curse as cruel as the evils that once resided in him

He had to end it,
For the alluring heaven he walked through felt like the most sinister hell with the torturous emotions of remorse and regret.
He was willing to die rather then remember

Through the pale skeletons that defined this place, he felt the dead watching,
He could sense their eyes, hear their lungs heaving,
And they attacked their killer with hatred

There was no chance of freedom.
Any opportunity of reobtaining his innocence was long gone.
The satisfaction of the plummet was indescribable
As it was for the dead to watch his demise

Maxim Anderson

A clock watcher

Most nights I'm a clock watcher
I just ponder, and factorize.
All the prime numbers up to 12:59
Are every night, before my eyes.
My speciality is the three square
I am patient as the digits appear
Like a friend I once knew long ago
Someone close, that loved me dear.
You would think there would be certain relief
Once the calculation is complete
Before the numbers change, I've done the maths
But all night keep pursuing my feat.
No sleep and it's 3:42
That's 2 squared, 19 and squared 3
Success and failure tossing inside my mind
As a ship on a restless sea.

Peter Levy

Charge

Charge your glass

Far higher than the sword- it can only pierce the sky above, whereas a chalice drinks in the mystical light of the darkening sky for the life below

With an elegance, more graceful tangents than the sweeping pen

Recognize that the chalice and the raised glass are as powerful as both the sword and the pen; as they have been carefully crafted for their purpose can be as uniting just as it can be cruel,

They have been your protector; a place for you to hide

Now you have the choice of freedom with new found breath,

And amongst those who hear your lips let wise words calm, unite and bless those too

Who makes a settlement with the days light passing, merging into the vivid darkness where dreams live?

Find an alliance between yourself and the one you hold at arm's length

For they may have been the very strength, as always, close to you without notice or tender

Charge your glass, your chalice; rest your sword and place your pen, look around at those who hear your words in celebration of companions and know that as time will change all or most of what is said

For this moment surrender to your friend, and see within their eyes the things they want to say to you

But never do, as your sword has been swift in striking before; and your pen has had a poison tip at times you'd rather ignore

Charge your glass with a salutation of honesty and worth; as opposed to the distance you built with walls of words you never dispersed

Raise above nothings and ignorance, settle into a knowing of acceptance and begin again, when the sky clears to lilac with light and the stars go back to another life

And your sword can only pierce the sky, as your pen is vital as are the words you need to recognise, that their delay puts you at an ever increasing distant slight

So, rather, Change and be true that is all anyone wants, just token and time in an anew that can be done.

Suzanne Siebert

For I love many

Never really is it the love of another, though we love for a while, the other.
It is also the love of life and everything it brings.
The love of doing and being.
The love of a project, a challenge that makes us grow that makes us feel again.
Like the love of a piece of artwork one is creating.
The love of doing your favourite thing whether it be work or play.
For who doesn't like to play?
The love of what we do best.
What comes naturally and what we can learn so we can stretch and grow.
To find who we truly are is just another love that we come across while looking for love and happiness.
With the love of the moment of creating.
Many loves to be had in this bountiful world of history, knowledge and creative endeavours of mind, heart and hands.

Rose Crane

Red is the colour of your eye

Red is the colour of your eye
as you lift the sword
Your heroic act Judith
goes not unnoticed by me
The tyrant Holofernes
is slain by a heroine's soft hand
and I, Donatello
salute you with my gift of bronze

Red is the colour of our revenge
as I, Artemesia
echoing your act
lift my brush and salute us both
with my gift of
victorious paint

S. G. Lanteri

www.ingramcontent.com/pod-product-compliance
Lightning Source LLC
Chambersburg PA
CBHW010244010526
44107CB00061B/2672